I0605816

THE LITTLE BOOK OF IRISH WIT & WISDOM

First published in 2026 by OH
An Imprint of HEADLINE PUBLISHING GROUP LIMITED

1

Cataloguing in Publication Data is available from the British Library

ISBN 978-1-03543-340-7

Compiled and written by Stella Caldwell
Editorial: Matt Tomlinson
Designed and typset in Warnock Pro by Tony Seddon
Project manager: Russell Porter
Production: Rachel Burgess
Printed and bound in Dubai

Headline's policy is to use papers that are natural, renewable and recyclable products and made from wood grown in well-managed forests and other controlled sources. The logging and manufacturing processes are expected to conform to the environmental regulations of the country of origin.

HEADLINE PUBLISHING GROUP LIMITED
An Hachette UK Company
Carmelite House, 50 Victoria Embankment, London EC4Y 0DZ

The authorised representative in the EEA is Hachette Ireland, 8 Castlecourt Centre, Dublin 15, D15 XTP3, Ireland (email: info@hbgi.ie)

www.headline.co.uk   www.hachette.co.uk

THE LITTLE BOOK OF

IRISH WIT & WISDOM

THE JOY OF LAUGHTER
AND THE MAGIC OF STORYTELLING

CONTENTS

INTRODUCTION

Ireland has long been a land of storytellers. From poets and playwrights to rebels and raconteurs, the Irish possess a rare and cherished gift – the ability to weave words into magic. Whether through poetry, song, jokes or casual conversation, they have a knack for turning a phrase that can invariably make us laugh, reflect or even bring a tear to the eye.

Within these pages, you'll discover sharp-tongued remarks from some of Ireland's greatest thinkers and writers, classic jokes that have stood the test of time, devilish insults (delivered with a twinkle in the eye), and expressions so uniquely Irish they couldn't have come from anywhere else. There are heartfelt blessings to warm the soul, toasts to raise a glass to, and wise words that may make you chuckle or ponder life's deeper truths. You'll also encounter curious facts and playful tidbits that celebrate the quirks, charm and enduring spirit of the Irish, showing how humour, warmth and hospitality are deeply engrained in the fabric of the culture.

This book is a tribute to the Irish love of language – to the easy banter between friends, the quick wit that can light up a room and the stories spun over pints that stretch long into the night. It's for anyone who has ever admired the lyrical flow of an Irish blessing or laughed at the sharp edge of an Irish insult. It honours the bonds of family and friendship, the warmth of a genuine welcome and the joy of sharing both words and a drink.

So, whether you're Irish by birth, heritage or simply at heart, pull up a chair, pour yourself a drop and enjoy the company. As the old saying goes, "There are no strangers here, only friends you haven't met yet."

Céad míle fáilte – a hundred thousand welcomes!

Chapter ONE

The Gift of the Gab

The Irish gift of the gab is more than just a knack for talking – it's an art form! It's the ability to weave words into tales, to spin a simple hello into an adventure and to leave listeners smiling long after the conversation ends.

Whether charming a crowd or simply bantering with a passer-by, the Irish know how to talk with warmth, wit and a dash of mischief.

“

I'm Irish. We think sideways.

”

Spike Milligan
Comedian, writer and actor (1918–2002)

“There is only one thing in the world worse than being talked about, and that is not being talked about.”

Oscar Wilde
Playwright, author and poet (1854–1900),
The Picture of Dorian Gray, 1890

Storytelling is woven into the fabric of Irish culture, passed down through generations around firesides and in bustling pubs – whether it's a humorous anecdote shared over a pint or an age-old myth involving fairies and ancient heroes.

The tale may entertain – but there's often a quiet wisdom tucked cleverly within the words.

"We Irish prefer embroideries to plain cloth. To us Irish, memory is a canvas – stretched, primed and ready for painting on. We love the 'story' part of the word 'history,' and we love it trimmed out with colour and drama, ribbons and bows. Listen to our tunes, observe a Celtic scroll: we always decorate our essence."

Frank Delaney
Novelist, journalist and broadcaster (1942–2017)

“A good storyteller never lets the facts get in the way.”

Dave Allen

Comedian, satirist and actor (1936–2005)

“

I was driving to Wicklow town and outside Wicklow town, there's a kind of country road and I came to a crossroad and there was one signpost and it had Wicklow on it and the other way was Wicklow. And there was a fella sitting there and I said, 'Does it make any difference?' And he said, 'Not to me it doesn't.'

”

Dave Allen

Comedian, satirist and actor (1936–2005)

Mick stops Paddy in Dublin and asks for the quickest way to Cork.

Paddy asks, "Are you on foot or in the car?"

"In the car," Mick replies.

"Well, that's the quickest way!" says Paddy.

Paddy and Murphy are walking down the road when Paddy finds a mirror. He picks it up, looks at it and says, "Jaysus, I know that face from somewhere..."

Murphy takes it, looks at it and says, "Of course you do, ya eejit – it's me!"

Jonathan Swift embodied the sharp, biting wit the Irish are celebrated for.

Best known as the author of *Gulliver's Travels* and *A Modest Proposal*, he used irony, satire and clever wordplay to expose political injustice and social absurdities.

"Every man desires to live long, but no man wishes to be old."

Jonathan Swift
Writer and satirist (1667–1745), *Gulliver's Travels*, 1726

"

Satire is a sort of glass wherein beholders do generally discover everybody's face but their own...

"

Jonathan Swift

Writer and satirist (1667–1745), *The Battle of the Books and Other Short Pieces*, 1704

"Fine words! I wonder where you stole them."

Jonathan Swift
Writer and satirist (1667–1745)

"Alas, I am dying beyond my means."

Oscar Wilde
Playwright, author and poet (1854–1900), allegedly uttered as he sipped champagne on his deathbed

“Birth was the death of him.”

Samuel Beckett
Playwright and author (1906–89),
Krapp's Last Tape, 1958

“

If you take too long in deciding what to do with your life, you’ll find you’ve done it.

”

George Bernard Shaw
Playwright and critic (1856–1950)

“The longer I live, the more convinced I am that this planet is used by other planets as a lunatic asylum.”

George Bernard Shaw
Playwright and critic (1856–1950)

The Blarney Stone is a block of limestone built into the battlements of Blarney Castle in County Cork.

According to legend, kissing it grants the gift of eloquence and persuasive speech – "the gift of the gab."

But it's not for the faint-hearted – visitors must lean backwards over a drop to reach it.

"

There is a stone there.
That whoever kisses.
Oh! he never misses
To grow eloquent.

"

Francis Sylvester Mahony (Father Prout)
Catholic priest, poet and journalist (1804–66)

“

Come forth, Lazarus!
And he came fifth
and lost the job.

”

James Joyce
Novelist, poet and literary critic (1882–1941),
Ulysses, 1922

"I am married to Beatrice Salkeld, a painter. We have no children, except me."

Brendan Behan
Poet, short story writer, novelist and playwright (1923–64)

“

A life spent making mistakes is not only more honourable, but more useful than a life spent doing nothing.

”

George Bernard Shaw
Playwright and critic (1856–1950)

“

The fickleness of the women I love is only equalled by the infernal constancy of the women who love me.

”

George Bernard Shaw
Playwright and critic (1856–1950)

Legendary playwright George Bernard Shaw was as famous for his sharp wit as for his brilliant plays.

In works like *Pygmalion* and *Man and Superman*, he challenged societal norms with clever dialogue and biting satire.

Never one to shy from a laugh, he once quipped, "I often quote myself. It adds spice to my conversation."

"What is life but a series of inspired follies? The difficulty is to find them to do. Never lose a chance: it doesn't come every day."

George Bernard Shaw
Playwright and critic (1856–1950), *Pygmalion*, 1913

"To love oneself is the beginning of a lifelong romance."

Oscar Wilde
Playwright, author and poet (1854–1900),
An Ideal Husband, 1895

“All the world’s a stage and most of us are desperately unrehearsed.”

Seán O’Casey
Playwright and memoirist (1880–1964)

“

You know your children are growing up when they stop asking you where they came from and refuse to tell you where they're going.

”

P. J. O'Rourke

Author, journalist and political satirist (1947–2022)

“The only thing that has to be finished by next Friday is next Thursday.”

Maureen Potter
Irish singer, actress and comedian (1925–2004)

Six Films

Filled with wit, wisdom and warmth, the following six films showcase Irish storytelling at its finest:

The Guard (2011)

A dark comedy where a small-town Galway guard with a sharp tongue partners with an uptight FBI agent.

In Bruges (2008)

This tale of two Irish hitmen trying (and failing) to lie low is equal parts hilarious and heartbreaking.

Intermission (2003)

Gritty and fast-paced, this Dublin ensemble film is full of awkward, offbeat characters and darkly funny moments.

Waking Ned Devine (1998)

A hilarious masterclass in understated Irish scheming and community spirit.

The Banshees of Inisherin (2022)

Darkly funny and heartbreakingly Irish, a quiet island feud becomes existentially ridiculous.

Sing Street (2016)

Set in 1980s Dublin, this film is bursting with heart, music and sly teenage humour.

Based on the novel by Roddy Doyle and directed by Alan Parker, *The Commitments* is a film that pulses with Dublin wit, charm and working-class swagger.

Brimming with chaotic characters, soulful ambition and sharp one-liners, it's a fast-talking, foul-mouthed celebration of music and the uniquely Irish gift of turning struggle into song.

Jimmy Rabbitte: "What do you play?"

Person in audition queue: "I used to play football in school."

Jimmy Rabbitte: "I mean, what instrument?"

Person in queue: "I don't."

Jimmy Rabbitte: "What are you doing here, then?"

Person in queue: "I saw everyone else lining up, so, uh – I thought you were selling drugs."

The Commitments, 1991

Chapter TWO

Céad Míle Fáilte

A THOUSAND WELCOMES

The Irish are known for their warmth, wit and hospitality – and a thousand other things. Quick with a joke, a drink or a shoulder to cry on, they face life with heart and spirit.

Whether laughing in a pub or dancing at a wake, being Irish means embracing the moment, lifting others up and finding the craic – wherever it hides.

If you're enough lucky to be Irish... you're lucky enough!

Irish proverb

"We Irish are too poetical to be poets; we are a nation of brilliant failures, but we are the greatest talkers since the Greeks."

Oscar Wilde
Playwright, author and poet (1854–1900)

Lady Gregory was the grand dame of Irish folklore and theatre – a woman with a sharp mind and an even sharper pen.

She collected stories of the people and helped put Irish voices on the world stage.

At a time when women were expected to stay quiet in the background, she made sure Ireland's stories spoke loud and clear – with wit, wisdom and a deep love for the old ways.

“

There’s more learning than is taught in books.

”

Lady Gregory

Dramatist, folklorist and theatre manager (1852–1932)

"

My number one choice is Guinness. My number two choice would be Guinness. My number three choice would have to be Guinness.

"

Peter O'Toole

Actor (1932–2013), when asked, "What's your favourite Irish food?"

“

Ireland is the only place in the world where procrastination takes on a sense of urgency.

”

Dave Allen,
Comedian, satirist and actor (1936–2005)

Spanish singer Julio Iglesias once appeared on television and used the word "mañana".

When the host asked him to explain its meaning, Iglesias replied, "It means the job will be done tomorrow... maybe the next day... perhaps next week, next month, next year. Who cares?"

The host turned to Irishman Shay Brennan – who was also on the show – and asked him if there was an equivalent term in Irish.

"No, in Ireland we don't have a word to describe that degree of urgency," replied Brennan.

As seen on caleythistleonline.com,
27 October 2007

"That's the Irish all over – they treat a joke as a serious thing and a serious thing as a joke."

Seán O'Casey
Irish dramatist and memoirist (1880–1964),
The Shadow of a Gunman, 1923

Legendary playwright, poet and socialite Oscar Wilde both dazzled and scandalized Victorian society.

With sharp humour and effortless charm, he exposed life's absurdities in brilliant one-liners and unforgettable plays.

His meteoric rise was matched by a tragic fall, but his wit endures – clever, cutting and endlessly quotable.

“

If one could only teach the English how to talk, and the Irish how to listen, society here would be quite civilized.

”

Oscar Wilde
Playwright, author and poet (1854–1900)

"I think there's something about the Irish experience – that we had to have a sense of humour or die."

Frank McCourt
Author and teacher (1930–2009)

"

I am, of course, directly descended from Brian Boru, the last king of Ireland, a fact certified by my mother and therefore beyond dispute. But as everybody else with a drop of Irish blood in his carcass is also a guaranteed descendant of the old billy goat, I am not overly arrogant because of this royal strain.

"

Preston Sturges

Playwright, screenwriter and film director (1898–1959)

"Dublin University contains the cream of Ireland – rich and thick."

Samuel Beckett
Playwright, author and former student at Trinity College Dublin (1906–1989)

“

The most important thing I would learn in school was that almost everything I would learn in school would be utterly useless. When I was 15, I knew the principal industries of the Ruhr Valley, the underlying causes of World War One and what Peig Sayers had for her dinner every day… What I wanted to know when I was 15 was the best way to chat up girls. That is what I still want to know.

”

Joseph O'Connor
Author (b.1963), *The Secret World of the Irish Male*, 1994

The farmer allows walkers across the field for free, but the bull charges.

Sign on a farm gate – a warm rural welcome

Out for lunch. If not back by five, out for dinner also.

Notice in an Irish shop window
(clearly run by someone with their priorities straight)

"

Being Irish, I have an abiding sense of tragedy which sustains me through temporary periods of joy.

"

W. B. Yeats

Poet, dramatist and writer (1865–1939)

“

An Irishman will always soften bad news, so that a major coronary is no more than ‘a bad turn’ and a near hurricane that leaves thousands homeless is ‘good drying weather.’

”

Hugh Leonard
Irish dramatist and writer (1926–2009)

"

When anyone asks me about the Irish character, I say look at the trees. Maimed, stark and misshapen, but ferociously tenacious.

"

Edna O'Brien
Irish novelist, playwright, poet and short story writer (1930–2024)

“

If it was raining soup, the Irish would go out with forks.

”

Brendan Behan
Poet, short story writer, novelist and playwright (1923–64)

How to Speak Irish

(Say it fast)

Whale
Oil
Beef
Hooked

The Irish gave
the bagpipes to
the Scots as a joke
– but the Scots
haven't seen the
joke yet.

Irish curses are a fiery blend of poetic flair and pointed wit – delivered with a smile that never quite reaches the eyes.

More than simple insults, they often invoke oddly specific misfortunes. "May your hens turn into foxes" or "Six horseloads of graveyard clay upon you" show that, in Ireland, even a curse is a blend of colourful humour and wild imagination.

May the curse of Mary Malone and her nine blind illegitimate children chase you so far over the hills of Damnation that the Lord himself can't find you."

Irish curse

Five Gaelic curses

Go n-ithe an cat thú, is go n-ithe an diabhal an cat.

"May the cat eat you, and may the devil eat the cat."

One of the most famous Irish curses – a two-for-one deal from hell!

Mallacht Chromaill ort!

"May the curse of Cromwell be upon you!"

Once the worst thing an Irish tongue could utter, this one's steeped in real historical rage.

Go ndeine an diabhal dréimire de cnámh do dhroma ag piocadh úll i ngairdín Ifrinn.

"May the devil make a ladder of your backbone [and] pluck apples in the garden of hell."

One of the darkest curses in Irish folklore – absolutely brutal!

An buinneach bhuí ort.

"May the yellow diarrhoea be upon you."

Vivid and visceral, a curse with flair!

Imeacht gan teacht ort!

"May you go without return!"

Not merely wishing misfortune, but the total severing of ties!

Chapter THREE

Sláinte!

In Ireland, a toast is more than a clink of glasses – it's a celebration of being together. Whether in a quiet kitchen or a crowded pub, the Irish raise a glass not just to drink, but to connection, conversation and craic.

This chapter honours the wit, warmth and wisdom that flow best when shared. Sláinte!

"The drink and I have been friends for so long, it would be a pity for me to leave without one last kiss."

Turlough O'Carolan
Harpist, singer and composer (1670–1738), reputed last words

“

A tavern is a place where they sell madness by the bottle.

”

Jonathan Swift
Writer and satirist (1667–1745)

"

O long life to the man who invented potheen –

Sure the Pope ought to make him a martyr –

If myself was this moment Victoria, the Queen,

I'd drink nothing but whiskey and wather.

"

Michael Moran, *aka* Zozimus
Balladeer (c.1794–1846), "In Praise of Potheen", mid-19th century

“

I only take a drink on two occasions – when I'm thirsty and when I'm not.

”

Brendan Behan

Poet, short story writer, novelist and playwright (1923–64)

Craic isn't just fun — it's the art of good company, sharp banter, a bit of madness and a lot of heart.

Found wherever people gather with stories and laughter, the craic flows best with music, mischief and perhaps a pint or two.

The secret? Never taking yourself too seriously – and never leaving too early…

Craic Levels

There's good craic and great craic – and then there's craic that goes off the rails...

Minus Craic – There's more fun to be had sitting in a waiting room.

Good Craic – Nothing too spectacular, but fun all the same.

Mighty Craic – Better than good – but not the best craic you've ever had.

Savage Craic – Great jokes and a great time.

Deadly Craic – A step above savage, but still not the pinnacle of craic.

The Craic was Ninety – The Everest of craic!

A priest is pulled over for speeding. As the traffic cop leans in to sniff his breath, he detects the unmistakable smell of alcohol.

The priest insists he's only been sipping water, but when the officer finds an empty wine bottle in the car, the holy man exclaims, "He's done it again!"

A man walks into a bar with a dog. He bets the bartender that the dog can talk and asks for free Guinness if he's right. The bartender agrees.

The man asks the dog, "What's on top of a house?" "Roof!" replies the dog. The bartender is unimpressed. The man asks again, "What's the texture of sandpaper?" "Rough!" says the dog. The bartender is still not convinced. Finally, the man asks, "Who's the greatest baseball player?" "Ruth!" replies the dog.

The bartender kicks them out.
Outside, the dog looks at the man and says, "Maybe I should have said DiMaggio?"

“

Stories,
like whiskey, must
be allowed to mature
in the cask.

”

Sean O’Faolain
Writer, commentator and critic (1900–91)

The truth comes out when the spirit goes in.

Irish proverb

"Logic, like whiskey, loses its beneficial effect when taken in too large quantities."

Lord Dunsany
Writer and dramatist (1878–1957)

Father O'Malley asks his parishioner, "Murphy, do you confess to drinking too much?"

Murphy replies, "No, Father, I never waste a drop!"

Irish whiskey is more than just a drink.

Steeped in centuries of tradition, it's a ritual of camaraderie, conversation and wit.

As an old Irish proverb goes, "What whiskey will not cure, there is no cure for!"

"

The light music of whiskey falling into a glass… an agreeable interlude!

"

James Joyce
Novelist, poet and literary critic (1882–1941)

Irish drinking toasts celebrate friendship, good fortune and laughter.

Here are five of the best:

May you be in heaven a half-hour before the devil knows you're dead!

Here's health to your enemies' enemies!

Here's to a long life and a merry one,
A quick death and an easy one,
A pretty girl and an honest one,
A cold pint and another one!

May your troubles be as few and as far apart as my grandmother's teeth!

May the roof above us never fall in, and may we friends beneath it never fall out!

"

The sacred pint alone can unbind the tongue...

"

James Joyce
Novelist, poet and literary critic (1882–1941),
Ulysses, 1920

May the lilt of Irish laughter,
Lighten every load.
May the mist of Irish magic,
Shorten every road...
And may all your friends
remember
All the favours you are owed!

Irish blessing

One of Ireland's literary giants, James Joyce revolutionized modern literature with his innovative style and sharp wit.

Best known for *Ulysses*, he masterfully captured the complexities of Dublin life.

His work not only reshaped the literary landscape but also showcased the depth, humour and character of Irish culture.

"

History… is a nightmare from which I am trying to awake.

"

James Joyce
Novelist, poet and literary critic (1882–1941),
Ulysses, 1920

"When things go wrong and will not come right,

Though you do the best you can,

When life looks black as the hour of night,

A pint of plain is your only man."

Flann O'Brien
Civil service official, novelist, playwright and satirist (1911–1966), *At Swim-Two-Birds*, 1939

An Irishman is desperately hunting for a parking space. He starts praying fervently, promising to give up Guinness if God helps him find a spot.

Lo and behold, a parking space suddenly appears.

Overwhelmed with gratitude, the man looks skyward and says, "Never mind, I found one!"

A man stumbles up to the only other patron in a bar and buys him a drink. "Where are you from?" he asks him.

"Ireland," comes the reply.

"I can't believe it," says the first man. "I'm from Ireland too! Let's drink to Ireland."

Then the first man asks, "Where in Ireland?"

"Dublin," the second man replies – and as the first man is also from there, they drink to Dublin...

“What school did you go to?” the first man asks.

“Saint Mary’s,” replies the second man. “I graduated in ‘62.”

“This is unbelievable!” the first man says. “I went to Saint Mary’s and I graduated in ‘62, too!”

In comes one of the regulars and sits down at the bar. “What’s been going on?” he asks the bartender.

“Nothing much,” replies the bartender. “The O’Malley twins are drunk again.”

Flann O'Brien, the pen name of Brian O'Nolan, was renowned for his talent for unravelling life's comic contradictions.

By day, a mild-mannered civil servant, O'Brien achieved fame for his novels *At Swim-Two-Birds, The Third Policeman* and *The Poor Mouth*.

Blending absurdity with biting satire, his work is distinguished by its colourful wordplay and mischievous subversion of literary conventions.

"Descartes spent far too much time in bed subject to the persistent hallucination that he was thinking. You are not free from a similar disorder."

Flann O'Brien
Civil service official, novelist, playwright and satirist (1911–66), *The Dalkey Archive*, 1964

Chapter FOUR

Through Laughter and Tears

The Irish have a gift for finding laughter in the middle of sorrow – and tears in the middle of joy. It's not about avoiding emotion – it's about embracing all of it, sometimes in the same breath.

From wakes that feel like parties to weddings that end in tears of laughter, the Irish heart beats to both rhythms.

“

Life does not cease to be funny when people die any more than it ceases to be serious when people laugh.

”

George Bernard Shaw
Playwright and critic (1856–1950)

“

The tears of the world are a constant quantity. For each one who begins to weep somewhere else another stops. The same is true of the laugh.

”

Samuel Beckett
Playwright and author (1906–89),
Waiting for Godot, 1952

Throughout history, Ireland has endured significant hardship – from famine and poverty to colonization and political struggle.

In the face of such adversity, humour became both a shield and a sword, a way to cope and carry on.

The Irish tradition of laughing both with and at hardship is about defying despair with a smile or a story.

May the good Lord take a liking to you, but not too soon.

Irish blessing

*May your pockets
be heavy and your heart
be light.
May good luck
pursue you each morning
and night.*

Irish blessing

A good laugh and a long sleep are the best cures in the doctor's book.

Irish proverb

The phrase "the luck of the Irish" originated in the US during the 19th-century gold and silver rushes.

Many Irish immigrants found great success in mining, leading to the idea that they were unusually lucky.

However, the phrase was often used sarcastically, implying that Irish success was mere luck rather than skill!

May your blessings
outnumber,
The Shamrocks that
grow,
And may trouble
avoid you,
Wherever you go.

Irish blessing

May luck be a friend
to ye,
And be with ye in all
yer days,
And may trouble be to ye,
A stranger, always.

Irish blessing

May those who love us, love us
And those who don't love us,
May God turn their hearts
And if he can't turn their hearts,
May he turn their ankles
So we will know them by their
limping!

Irish blessing

An Irishman walks into a bar and orders three pints of Guinness.

He takes a sip from the first, then the second and finally the third – and repeats the routine all over again.

The bartender asks what he's up to. "I have two brothers, one in New York and one in Sydney," he replies. "Since I can't drink with them, I order three pints of Guinness and take a sip in turn from each one – and they do the same in New York and Sydney…

Each day, the Irishman returns to the bar and orders his three pints of Guinness – and everyone gets to know his story.

Then one day, he walks in and orders just two pints.

The bar goes silent. Finally, the bartender approaches him and says, "On behalf of everyone here, I want to extend our condolences on the passing of your brother..."

The Irishman replies, "Oh, no, it's not that! It's just that I've given up the drink!"

Dublin-born Samuel Beckett was a master of bleak brilliance.

With dry wit and razor-sharp insight, he explored the absurdity of life, famously writing *Waiting for Godot* – a play of which it was famously said "nothing happens – twice."

Awarded the Nobel Prize in Literature in 1969, Beckett remains a towering figure in modern literature.

“You’re on earth, there’s no cure for that!”

Samuel Beckett

Playwright and author (1906–89), *Endgame*, 1957

"

The hallway of every man's life is paced with pictures; pictures gay and pictures gloomy, all useful, for if we be wise, we can learn from them a richer and braver way to live.

"

Sean O'Casey
Playwright and memoirist (1880–1964)

“

Life is a journey that must be travelled, no matter how bad the road and accommodations.

”

Oliver Goldsmith
Novelist, playwright, poet and physician (1728–74)

An Irish funeral is a unique blend of sorrow and celebration.

While the grief of loss is of course deeply felt, families and friends come together to share touching stories, fond memories and often a bit of humour.

At the wake, both tears and laughter flow freely, honouring the deceased with love, remembrance and a sense of community.

“

The terrible thing about dying over in Ireland is you miss your own wake. It’s the best day of your life. You’ve paid for everything and you can’t join in. Mind you, if you did you’d be drinking on your own.

”

Dave Allen

Comedian, satirist and actor (1936–2005)

"I knew if I waited around long enough something like this would happen."

George Bernard Shaw
Playwright and critic (1856–1950),
written as his own epitaph

Beneath this stone lies
Katherine my wife

In death my comfort, and my
plague through life

Oh liberty! but soft I
must not boast

She'll haunt me else, by jingo,
with her ghost.

Epitaph from a Belfast cemetery

Chapter FIVE

Kith and Kin

In Ireland, family isn't just blood – it's the neighbours who raised you, the cousins who feel like siblings and the strangers who become kin over a pint. The Irish celebrate each other loudly, mourn in style and always know who your granny was.

Whether by blood or banter, Irish bonds run deep – and once you're in, you'll never drink alone (or get away with anything).

"Think where man's glory most begins and ends,
And say my glory was I had such friends."

W. B. Yeats
Poet, dramatist and writer (1865–1939),
"The Municipal Gallery Revisited", 1939

“

True friends stab you in the front.

”

Oscar Wilde

Playwright, author and poet (1854–1900)

Deeply rooted in tradition, Irish blessings are cherished expressions of warmth and goodwill, frequently sprinkled with humour.

Often shared during significant life events such as birthdays and weddings, these sayings offer a delightful blend of wit and sharp observation.

May you have warm
words on a cold evening,

a full moon on a dark
night,

and the road downhill
all the way to your door.

Irish blessing

May the road rise up to meet you.

May the wind be always at
your back.

May the sun shine warm upon
your face,

the rains fall soft upon your fields.

And until we meet again,
may God hold you in the palm of
His hand.

Irish blessing

May you live as long as you want, and never want as long as you live.

Irish blessing

A man loves his sweetheart the most, his wife the best, but his mother the longest.

Irish proverb

“

Marriage: When two people are under the influence of the most violent, most insane, most delusive and most transient of passions, they are required to swear that they will remain in that excited, abnormal and exhausting condition continuously until death do them part.

”

George Bernard Shaw
Playwright and critic (1856–1950)

"

The real genius for love lies not in getting into – but getting out of love.

"

George Moore
Novelist, poet and playwright (1852–1933)

“In married life, three is company and two is none.”

Oscar Wilde
Playwright, author and poet (1854–1900),
The Importance of Being Earnest, 1895

An Irish wedding is less about perfection and more about celebration – loud, lively and lasting longer than anyone planned!

Rain is a blessing, speeches run long and someone's uncle will sing.

Vows are heartfelt, the cake might collapse and love is sealed with a toast – or five.

Sláinte chuig na fir agus go maire na mná go deo!

Health to the men and may the women live forever.

Irish blessing

“

If I had not married, I should not have learned the quick enrichment of sentences that one gets in conversation; had I not been widowed I should not have found the detachment of mind the leisure for observation, necessary to give insight into character, to express and interpret it… Loneliness made me rich.

”

Lady Gregory
Dramatist, folklorist and theatre manager
(1852–1932)

“

Marriage is the triumph of imagination over intelligence. Second marriage is the triumph of hope over experience.

”

Oscar Wilde
Playwright, author and poet (1854–1900)

At a wedding ceremony, the priest asks if anyone knows of any reason why the bride and groom should not be joined in holy matrimony. If so, they must speak now – or forever hold their peace.

A beautiful, young woman carrying a child stands up and slowly starts to make her way towards the priest...

Everything quickly turns to chaos.

The bride slaps the groom, the groom's mother faints and the ushers start giving each other looks, wondering how to save the situation.

The priest asks the woman, "Can you tell us why you came forward? What do you have to say?"

The woman replies, "We can't hear at the back."

Six Irish Novels

The following novels – by turns, witty lyrical and profound – embody the very best of Irish storytelling, steeped in history, humour and a deep sense of place.

"Ulysses" by James Joyce

It's complicated, sure, but this landmark of modernist literature is filled with dazzling wordplay, and offers an affectionate satire of Dublin life.

"An Béal Bocht" ("The Poor Mouth") by Flann O'Brien

This satirical jab at Gaelic revival literature is hilariously absurd.

"Poguemahone" by Patrick McCabe

A wild, poetic and darkly funny stream-of-consciousness novel.

"The Spinning Heart" by Donal Ryan

Laced with a dry, bleak humour, this sharply observed novel captures the unravelling of a community in post-crash Ireland.

"Milkman" by Anna Burns

Inventive and bleakly funny, this Booker-Prize-winner uses a unique voice to capture the tension and claustrophobia of life during the Troubles.

"Skippy Dies" by Paul Murray

As hilarious as it is heartbreaking, this exuberant novel explores adolescence in a Dublin boys' school.

“A man is already half in love with any woman who listens to him.”

Brendan Behan
Poet, short story writer, novelist and playwright (1923–64)

“

Friendship is a disinterested commerce between equals; love an abject intercourse between tyrants and slaves.

”

Oliver Goldsmith
Novelist, playwright, poet and physician (1728–74)

Carrying the wisdom of centuries, Irish proverbs have been passed down through storytelling and even woven into ancient laws.

With roots in Ireland's rich oral tradition and bardic culture, many proverbs have survived for more than a thousand years.

They offer timeless truths and insights into human behaviour – always with an Irish flair.

*Is fearr an tsláinte
ná na táinte.*

Health is better
than wealth.

Irish proverb

Five Pithy Proverbs

Cuir síoda ar ghabhar ach is gabhar i gcónaí é.

Dress a goat in silk – and it's still a goat.

An té a luíonn le madaí, eiroidh sé le dearnaid.

He who lies down with dogs, gets up with fleas.

Is minic a bhris béal duine a shrón.

Many a time a man's mouth broke his nose.

An rud is annamh is iontach.

The thing that is rare is wonderful.

Ar scáth a chéile a mhaireann na daoine.

We all live in each other's shadow.

A friend is known in hardship.

Irish proverb

May the
hinges of our
friendship
never
grow rusty.

Irish toast

The Irish Mammy is a legend in her own right.

Fiercely loving and protective, she'll always tell you how it is – whether you like it or not.

From questioning your life choices to chiding you for not eating enough (even when you've had more potatoes than anyone else), she has an opinion on everything – and she's never afraid to share it!

Five Irish Mammy-isms

"Say a Hail Mary or two and you'll be fine." – Sadly, this isn't foolproof.

"I'm not one to gossip, but..." – Followed by 10 minutes of Grade A gossip.

"Don't be acting the maggot." – A classic warning that nonsense will not be tolerated.

"It was a lovely funeral, all the same." – An Irish mammy knows a good funeral when she sees one.

"Jesus, Mary and Joseph... what were you thinking?" – Usually reserved for big life decisions and dodgy haircuts.

The family that has no skeleton in the cupboard has buried it instead.

Irish proverb

“

If you cannot get rid of the family skeleton, you may as well make it dance.

”

George Bernard Shaw
Playwright and critic (1856–1950)

"Good heavens! How marriage ruins a man! It's as demoralizing as cigarettes and far more expensive."

Oscar Wilde
Playwright, author and poet (1854–1900)

Murphy tells Quinn that his wife is driving him to the drink.

"Aw, now, isn't that a stroke of luck," replies Quinn. "Molly makes me walk."

"

It is very easy to endure the difficulties of one's enemies. It is the successes of one's friends that are hard to bear.

"

Oscar Wilde
Playwright, author and poet (1854–1900)

A kind word never broke anyone's mouth.

Irish proverb

Chapter SIX

A Pint of Wit

AND A DROP OF WISDOM

In Ireland, humour flows as freely as the finest pint while wisdom is often tucked beneath a well-timed quip. This chapter celebrates the Irish knack for mixing sharp wit with deep insight.

Whether it's a clever turn of phrase or a quiet reflection, the following pages raise a glass to both the laughter and lessons that life offers.

“

’Tis an old maxim in the schools,

that flattery’s the food of fools;

yet now and then your men of wit

will condescend to take a bit.

”

Jonathan Swift

Writer and satirist (1667–1745)

“

He was a bold man, that first ate an oyster.

”

Jonathan Swift

Writer and satirist (1667–1745), *A Complete Collection of Genteel and Ingenious Conversation*, 1738

Writer and playwright Oliver Goldsmith (1730–1774) is best known for works such as *The Vicar of Wakefield* and *The Deserted Village*.

His writing is characterized by its warmth, humour and social critique.

Goldsmith's legacy endures as a masterful storyteller and insightful observer of life, blending sharp wit with keen observations on human nature.

“Handsome is that handsome does.”

Oliver Goldsmith
Novelist, playwright, poet and physician (1728–74),
The Vicar of Wakefield, 1766

“

‘What is whiter than snow?’ he said.
‘The truth,’ said Grania.

‘What is the best colour?’ said Finn.
‘The colour of childhood,’ said she.

‘What is hotter than fire?’
‘The face of a hospitable man when he sees a stranger coming in, and the house empty.’

‘What has a taste more bitter than poison?’ ‘The reproach of an enemy.’...

‘What is best for a champion?’
‘His doings to be high, and his pride to be low.’

‘What is the best of jewels?’ ‘A knife.’

‘What is sharper than a sword?’ ‘The wit of a woman between two men.’

‘What is quicker than the wind?’ said Finn then. ‘A woman’s mind,’ said Grania.

And indeed, she was telling no lie when she said that.

”

Lady Gregory

Dramatist, folklorist and theatre manager (1852–1932), *Gods and Fighting Men*, 1902

Irish insults are a fine art – witty, biting and usually followed by a laugh. Here are five to get your teeth into...

"Eejit" – A lovable idiot. Harmless, but definitely not flattering.

"Gobshite" – Someone who talks nonsense or acts the fool.

"Cute hoor" – A sly, crafty person who gets what they want, often by bending the rules.

"He's not the full shilling" – Suggesting someone's a bit dim.

"You're as thick as manure – but only half as useful." – Not exactly a compliment!

Sean's wife was in the Rotunda Hospital, ready to give birth to their first child.

When they arrived, the nurse asked, "How dilated is she, Sir?"

Sean replied, "Delighted? She's over the feckin' moon!"

The Irish have a unique talent for poking fun at priests, nuns and their own Catholic guilt – all while turning up for Mass on Sunday.

From whispered confessions to overzealous rosary-clutchers, faith and farce often go hand in hand.

During Mass, a priest says, "Whoever puts the most in the collection plate today can choose the next three hymns!"

After the plate goes around, he sees a €50 note. "Ah, such generosity! Who gave this?"

A shy old lady raises her hand. "Wonderful," says the priest. "Now, which hymns would you like?"

She smiles and points across the church, "Him... him... and him."

In Ireland, it's often said that if you don't like the weather, just wait five minutes – it'll change its mind.

And remember, it's not bad weather, just character-building...

Sure, isn't all that rain grand for the grass? (That's Irish optimism at its finest!)

Irish Weather Expressions

"It's a soft day, thank God."

(It's raining, but gently... so no harm done.)

“There’s great drying out.”

(Often said as rain lashes the windows – possibly ironic, possibly delusional.)

“Sure, it’s only a grand bit of sideways rain.”

(Sideways rain, driven by wind, is a regular feature…)

“You’d be soaked to the bone – and that’s just walking to the kitchen.”

(Indoor weather reports are a real thing in Ireland!)

"He knows nothing; and he thinks he knows everything. That points clearly to a political career."

George Bernard Shaw
Playwright and critic (1856–1950), *Major Barbara*, 1905

“

I was elected by the women of Ireland, who instead of rocking the cradle, rocked the system.

”

Mary Robinson

Irish politician (b.1944), who served as Ireland's first female president

"

A man is original when he speaks the truth that has always been known to all good men.

"

Patrick Kavanagh
Poet and novelist (1904–67)

"Poetry is what we do to break bread with the dead."

Seamus Heaney
Poet and playwright (1939–2013)

One of Ireland's best-loved TV shows, *Father Ted* – which aired across three series from 1995 to 1998 – blended absurd humour with sharp social commentary.

Set on the fictional Craggy Island, it followed Father Ted Crilly and his eccentric colleagues as they navigated bizarre situations with hilarious consequences.

“

It’s nice to have a nun around. Gives the place a bit of glamour.

”

Father Dougal McGuire

"Grant Unto Him Eternal Rest", *Father Ted*, 1995

"My father had a profound influence on me, he was a lunatic."

Spike Milligan
Comedian, writer and actor (1918–2002)

“We are all in the gutter, but some of us are looking at the stars.”

Oscar Wilde
Playwright, author and poet (1854–1900),
Lady Windermere's Fan, 1892

"

Youth is wasted on the young.

"

George Bernard Shaw
Playwright and critic (1856–1950)

“

Our greatest glory is not in never falling, but in rising every time we fall.

”

Oliver Goldsmith

Novelist, playwright, poet and physician (1728–74)

"I never put off till tomorrow what I can do the day after."

Oscar Wilde
Playwright, author and poet (1854–1900)

“What do I know of man’s destiny? I could tell you more about radishes.”

Samuel Beckett
Playwright and author (1906–1989)

"

Money does not make you happy but it quiets the nerves.

"

Seán O'Casey
Playwright and memoirist (1880–1964)

"Man is least himself when he talks in his own person. Give him a mask, and he will tell you the truth."

Oscar Wilde

Playwright, author and poet (1854–1900)

Advertisment in
the paper:

"Tree Fellers Wanted"

"Look here," says Paddy.
"If we get Donal to join us, we
could do that."

Q: What's the difference between an Irish wedding and an Irish wake?

A: One pint of Guinness

A dog owns nothing, yet is seldom dissatisfied.

Irish proverb

You'll never plough a field by turning it over in your mind.

Irish proverb

Leprechauns are mischievous little tricksters of Irish folklore — cobblers by trade, hoarders of gold and masters of escape.

Catch one, they say, and he'll grant you three wishes... if you're lucky!

Five (Terrible) Leprechaun Jokes

What do you call a leprechaun that doesn't want to do anything?

A lepre-can't

What kind of pictures do leprechauns take?

Elfies

How did the leprechaun get to the Moon?

In a sham-rocket

Why do leprechauns make terrible comedians?

Their jokes are always a wee bit short

What did the baby leprechaun find at the end of the rainbow?

A potty gold

Customer: "In six days, do you hear me, in six days, God made the world... And you are not bloody well capable of making me a pair of trousers in three months!"

Tailor: "But my dear Sir, my dear Sir, look – at the world – and look – at my trousers."

Samuel Beckett
Playwright and author (1906–1989),
Endgame, 1957

"You don't stop laughing when you grow old, you grow old when you stop laughing."

George Bernard Shaw
Playwright and critic (1856–1950)